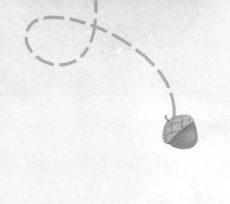

Presented to

From

Date

© 2003, 2004, 2006 Mary Manz Simon. ©2003, 2004, 2006 Standard Publishing, Cincinnati, Ohio.
A division of Standex International Corporation. All rights reserved. First Virtues® is a registered trademark of Standard Publishing.
Printed in Singapore. Project editor: Jennifer Holder. Design: Robert Glover, Suzanne Jacobson. Scripture quoted from the
HOLY BIBLE, Contemporary English Version. Copyright ©1995 by American Bible Society. Used by permission.
ISBN 0-7847-1848-2

12 11 10 09 08 07 06 9 8 7 6 5 4 3 2 1

First Virtues® for Toddlers

written by Dr. Mary Manz Simon

Standard®
PUBLISHING
Bringing The Word to Life

Cincinnati, Ohio

Contents

People may be kind to you
If you're kind and loving, too!

Kitty Shows Kindness

illustrated by Linda Clearwater

Kitty, Kitty,
share today,
what the Bible
has to say…

Kindness means
I am aware
when someone needs
help and care.

If I see
someone in need,
that's when I do
a kind deed.

14

15

When the sun
is burning hot,
I show friends
a shady spot.

When someone
is scared at night,
I purr,
"Everything's all right."

If I'm tempted
to be cruel,
I recall
the Golden Rule.

21

People may be
kind to you,
if you're kind
and loving, too.

23

God is very
kind to me.
He cares for me
tenderly.

God shows me
what I should do.
Do you show
such kindness, too?

"Be kind to everyone."
2 Timothy 2:24

27

Know what's false and what is true.

What does honest mean to you?

Piglet Tells the Truth

illustrated by Dorothy Stott

Piglet, Piglet,
share today,
what the Bible
has to say...

31

When I say
I will be true,
that means
I won't lie to you.

33

If I make
a great big mess,
I'll be honest
and confess.

35

I will not steal
from a store.
I will pay
at the front door.

APPLES
25¢

25¢

I will keep
my promise true.
That is being
honest, too.

If I say,
"I'll clean my room,"
I will use
a mop and broom.

40

When God tells me,
"I love you,"
those three words
are honest, too.

42

43

Oink, oink!
I will say and do
what I think
and know is true.

45

Know what's false
and what is true.
What does honest
mean to you?

"I have chosen the way of truth."
Psalm 119:30

47

God is love. He cares for you.
Will you share his love now, too?

Bunny Loves Others

illustrated by Dorothy Stott

Bunny, Bunny,
share today,
what the Bible
has to say...

God is love.
It all starts there,
with our Father's
gentle care.

Then because
God loves me so,
I want all
the world to know!

55

Love shows in
my smiling face,
when I fill
a flower vase.

57

When I bring
a gift to share,
that will show
my love and care.

This is one thing
that I know:
it is fun
to watch love grow.

And to show
that I care, too,
I will whisper,
"I love you."

63

God shows love
to me each day.
That is why
I smile and say...

65

God is love.
He cares for you.
Will you share
his love now, too?

"Love God and love each other!"
1 John 4:21

67

You go first, ahead of me.
I will stand here patiently!

Duckling Is Patient

illustrated by Linda Clearwater

Duckling, Duckling,
share today,
what the Bible
has to say...

71

Patience means
that I am fine
standing in
a long, long line.

73

You go first,
ahead of me.
I will stand here
patiently.

Good things come
to those who wait.
When I'm patient,
I feel great.

Patience, patience,
wait my turn.
This is one thing
I must learn.

I admit
it's hard to wait,
if my mother's
running late.

But I know
that God helps me
wait for her
so patiently.

When I'm feeling
anxious, too,
God is here
to help me through.

85

I can count on God,
it's true.
Did you know that
you can, too?

"It's smart to be patient."
Proverbs 14:29

God forgives, so I can, too.
That is what I try to do!

Tiger Forgives

illustrated by Linda Clearwater

Tiger, Tiger,
share today,
what the Bible
has to say...

To forgive means
move on past.
Don't let angry
feelings last.

93

If a friend
steps on my toe,
I will pardon her,
you know.

When someone
won't share a toy,
I forgive
that girl or boy.

Then we have
a brand new start.
I feel kindness
in my heart.

99

"**I** forgive"
are words I say
almost every
single day.

If a friend
does not play fair,
I forgive
to show I care.

103

God forgives,
so I can, too.
That is what
I try to do.

"**I** forgive,"
God says to you.
Are those words
that you say, too?

"Forgive others,
and God will forgive you."
Luke 6:37

When does friendship really start?
When you share love from your heart.

Puppy Makes Friends

illustrated by Kathy Couri

Puppy, Puppy,
share today,
what the Bible
has to say…

Friendly means
to understand
when a person
needs a hand.

When does friendship
really start?
When you share love
from your heart.

Playing ball
is lots more fun
when I'm not
the only one.

If a friend
falls in a race,
I will wipe tears
from his face.

I show I am
friendly, too,
when I talk
with someone new.

121

My new friend
begins to smile,
after we
have played awhile.

When I'm friendly,
then I share,
for that shows
I really care.

God is always
there for you.
He wants to be
your friend, too.

"A friend is always a friend."
Proverbs 17:17

I say "Thank you" every day
for the good that comes my way.

Squirrel Says Thank You

illustrated by Kathy Couri

Squirrel, Squirrel,
share today,
what the Bible
has to say…

131

I say "Thank you"
every day
for the good
that comes my way.

I count blessings:
one, two, three.
God gives such
great things to me.

Ice cream tastes
so nice and sweet.
I thank God
for this cold treat.

I thank God
for big, tall trees,
and the cooling
autumn breeze.

And when snowflakes
flutter by,
I thank God
I'm warm and dry.

I am glad
for family, too--
people who say
"I love you."

143

These are blessings
big and small.
Thank you, God,
for giving all.

145

God shares
each of these with me.
I say "Thank you"
gratefully.

146

147

God would like us to obey
rules at home, at school, and play.

Bear
Obeys

illustrated by Linda Clearwater

Little Bear, please
share today,
what the Bible
has to say...

Rules and laws
say what to do.
They are good
for me and you.

When you do
what those rules say,
then you show
that you obey.

No Litter

155

I will wait
for the green light.
I obey,
for that is right.

157

If the rule is
share the toys,
I will share
with girls and boys.

If my mom says,
"Wait for me,"
I will stand
here patiently.

God would like
us to obey
rules at home,
at school, and play.

When I hear
"It's time for bed,"
I lay down
my sleepy head.

God will listen
as you pray.
He will help
you to obey.

"I obey your law."
Psalm 119:55

167

Joy comes from the inside out.

"God loves me," I want to shout.

Lamb Is Joyful

illustrated by Linda Clearwater

Little Lamb,
please share today,
what the Bible
has to say...

Joy's a gift
from God above.
With it, I feel
peace and love.

173

Joy comes from
the inside out.
"God loves me,"
I want to shout.

When my bubbles
reach the sky,
I feel joy
as they float by.

177

If I get
a brand new toy,
then I
overflow with joy.

If I get
a funny card,
joy comes when
I laugh real hard.

Sad times come
and sad times go--
this is something
that I know.

Soon the sadness
goes away,
and the joy
is here to stay.

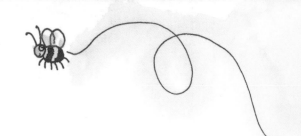

Show your joy because it's true. You can smile for God loves you!

"Always be joyful."
1 Thessalonians 5:16

186

When I get a brand new book,
I will say, "Here, take a look."

Lion Can Share

illustrated by Phyllis Harris

Lion, Lion,
share today,
what the Bible
has to say...

191

God's Word says
that we should share
from our hearts,
to show we care.

193

If I have some
coins to spend,
I can share them
with my friend.

I will share
my many toys.
I give some
to girls and boys.

When I get
a brand new book,
I will say,
"Here, take a look."

If I see
you're hungry, too,
I will share
my snack with you.

And if someone
looks so sad,
I share smiles
to make him glad.

For I care
from inside out.
That's what
sharing's all about.

God gives me
so much to share.
How do you show
that you care?

"Be generous and willing to share."
1 Timothy 6:18

206

When I say, "How do you do?"
I reach out to shake hands, too.

Panda Is Polite

illustrated by Linda Clearwater

Panda, Panda,
share today,
what the Bible
has to say...

Have good manners
every day,
when you work
and when you play.

When I say,
"How do you do?"
I reach out
to shake hands, too.

I will listen
quietly,
then you'll do
the same for me.

When I smile
and say, "Thank you!"
that shows
my good manners, too.

When I am
about to sneeze,
that's when I say,
"Tissue, please."

I will hold
the door for you,
so that you can
walk right through.

I know that
when I'm polite,
I am doing
what is right.

225

Manners say,
"I care for you."
Can you show
good manners, too?

"Show proper respect to everyone."
1 Peter 2:17

I will always try my best.
I'll work hard to pass a test.

Koala Does His Best

illustrated by Phyllis Harris

Koala, Koala,
share today,
what the Bible
has to say...

Do your best
in everything,
if you jump
or run or sing.

When I'm trying
something new,
it may take
a while to do.

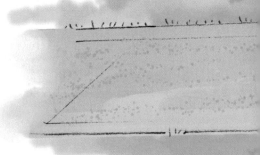

235

If I'm learning
how to read,
I will practice
to succeed.

I will always
try my best.
I'll work hard
to pass a test.

I won't leave
a job half done,
even when
it's not much fun.

If I want to
play a song,
I must practice
hard and long.

243

When I do
so well, you see,
God is also
proud of me.

Do your best
is what I say.
What did you
do well today?

"Hard work is worthwhile."
Proverbs 14:23

247

Help your toddler build godly character!

Kindness

The Scripture "Be kind to everyone" (2 Timothy 2:24) poses a challenge during the early years. A young child sees himself at the center of the world, so the very act of being helpful, caring, or compassionate requires a child to reach out to others. The concept of kindness begins to have real-world meaning when the word *kind* is attached to specific actions. For example, "That was kind of you to invite John to play." Even when a young child repeatedly experiences or shows kindness, he will not understand until he's older that being kind makes things better for everyone.

Catch your child being kind when he or she:

- draws a picture for a sick friend
- shops for a birthday present
- reaches out to hold a friend's hand
- picks up trash that missed the wastebasket
- pets an animal gently

Love

The heartfelt love a young child experiences from people around him reflects God's incredible love for us. The endearing phrase "I love you" is frequently included in daily conversations with a child or as part of a nighttime routine, but the intense emotion behind those words comes directly from the Bible. "We can love others because God first loved us" clearly identifies the original source of love. The depth of our feeling for God is reflected in the way we treat others. Every day, a child not only sees how we put that love into action, but receives the reassuring message that he is loved.

Catch your child showing love when he or she:

- spontaneously gives a hug
- tells someone "I love you"
- polishes an apple to give away
- "reads" a book to someone who is sick
- gets a diaper for a baby

Thankfulness

An infant is totally dependent on others. That's why it's natural that young children expect their needs—and sometimes their desires—to be met. After all, they've grown up being served. As a result, gratitude must be intentionally modeled and taught. There are clear benefits for everyone: when a child observes people who notice God's goodness, a child may start to thank God for the little things of life adults often take for granted. As a young child discovers the wonders of the world—the color of an autumn leaf or the fragrance of a pumpkin pie—parents can be grateful that we are allowed to see the world through the eyes of a thankful child.

Catch your child being thankful when he or she:

- counts three good things that happen today
- looks for something cheery when the weather is gloomy
- finds the brightest star in the night sky
- accepts a gift graciously
- prays "thank you, God, for today"

Truthfulness

During the early years, a young child learns to distinguish between fact and fiction. He is taught to define a lie as something that is not true. He learns it's good to be honest. However, this understanding of truthfulness occurs gradually. In the meantime, a child might pretend, exaggerate, cover up a mistake, or make false promises. When this happens, encourage your child to stop for a moment, think about what he's going to say, and then remember to be honest. This approach gives a child the time and opportunity to make a conscious decision to "[choose] the way of truth" (Psalm 119:30).

Catch your child being truthful when he or she:

- recognizes what is true and what is false
- explains "I will tell you a pretend story" when speaking from his imagination
- returns a candy bar that wasn't paid for to the store
- keeps a promise
- admits "I made a mistake"

Obedience

An adult who sets rules gives a child freedom: a child is free within the limits. He knows exactly how far he can go; there's no uncertainty. The problem comes when a child tests those limits. This usually happens when children are tired, hungry, or thirsty. To encourage compliance, boundaries should be clear and consistent. This is especially important when children have multiple caregivers or participate in activities with varied boundaries. Of course, it's easiest for children to obey the rules when adults in their lives model the core biblical principle "I obey your law" (Psalm 119:55).

Catch your child being obedient when he or she:

- wears a bike helmet even in hot weather
- takes turns when playing a game
- crosses the street at the light with an adult
- follows a rule at grandma's that's different from a rule at home
- fastens the seat belt without a reminder

Patience

A young child has not developed an understanding of time and space. Because he doesn't know that "tomorrow" is only twenty-four hours away, waiting for a new baby or a birthday might seem like forever. To help a child learn "it's smart to be patient," begin by asking your child to wait for brief periods of time. Let him watch sand sift through a small hourglass or egg timer while he's waiting for his bread to toast. Or, make a simple paper plate clock, using a brad to attach movable hands, so the child can make time march ahead by matching his clock to the kitchen clock. Time will move more quickly when a child is mentally and physically active.

Catch your child being patient when he or she:

- keeps a birthday present a secret until the party
- waits in line without making a fuss
- avoids interrupting
- sits quietly in the car when you're in a traffic jam
- plants a seed, waters it, and waits for a plant to grow

Friendliness

Developmentally, most young children go through specific weeks when they deal with separation anxiety. That's why it's totally normal for even an outgoing child to hide behind an adult instead of greeting people.

Societally, we live in a risk-aware world. A valid concern for "stranger danger" has made some parents hesitant to encourage a child's sociability. Yet within safe spaces, children should learn how to make a friend, be a friend, and keep a friend. That will lead to a growing appreciation for the Scriptural truth "A friend is always a friend" (Proverbs 17:17).

Catch your child being friendly when he or she:

- asks someone "how do you feel?"
- is the first to smile
- invites a child to play
- holds a swing steady while a child climbs on
- gets a tissue for someone who sneezed

Forgiveness

A child who says "I forgive you" and then moves beyond the difficult situation shows an understanding of forgiveness. Some young children have a relatively easy time forgiving and forgetting. However, this two-step process must be repeated many times before a child recognizes the cleansing action that characterizes this virtue. Some parents find that saying "I forgive you and so does Jesus" is a good way to remind a child that Jesus said, "Forgive others, and God will forgive you" (Luke 6:37).

Catch your child showing forgiveness when he or she:

- says "I'm sorry"
- rebuilds a tower back up after a child knocks it over
- hugs someone who apologized
- is kind to a child who cut to the front of the line
- eats the peanut butter sandwich after grandma forgets he doesn't like peanut butter

Sharing

Generations of parents have been amused by a baby who gives away a toy and then snatches it back a moment later. Yet this early behavior sets the stage for learning to give freely and forever, for that defines true sharing. It is easiest for a child to share when there is an abundance to give away: for example, a child who passes a tray of cookies when there are more than enough for everyone experiences the joy of giving. In this situation, the child will be affirmed for his generous spirit. Eventually, a child will learn to give from the heart without expecting to receive anything in return. At that point, he will begin to embrace the Scriptural truth to "be generous and willing to share" (1 Timothy 6:18).

Catch your child sharing when he or she:

- scoots over to let another child see the pictures in a book
- takes turns using a single piece of sidewalk chalk
- breaks a cookie in half for a friend
- donates a toy to a needy family
- thanks God for opportunities to give

Excellence

Children are growing up in a world where fast is good but hyperspeed is better. So how can a young child embrace the proverb that "hard work is worthwhile" (Proverbs 14:23)? Among young children who think concretely, examples often speak louder than words. Help a child smooth the covers on the bed, then stand back with him to admire the extra bit of work. Make a game of collecting all the blocks from the floor before joining your child in an ear-splitting cheer for the great job. When we set high but developmentally appropriate standards, children will stretch to reach them, especially if we stand alongside to help.

Catch your child doing his best when he or she:

- pulls all the weeds in a long garden row
- returns a book to the shelf instead of leaving it on the floor
- practices—again and again—kicking the soccer ball
- brushes to get out all the tangles
- lines up shoes under the bed

Courtesy

The biblical command to "show proper respect to everyone" (1 Peter 2:17) highlights the virtue that defines polite behavior: a child must learn to be respectful. Traditional courtesies that reflect respect can be practiced repeatedly during everyday situations. Sneezing into a tissue, washing hands before eating, and opening mail only addressed to you are common examples. However, a child will not learn these courtesies simply because they have been transferred from previous generations. Polite behavior must be embraced by adults today and taught to this generation of children, beginning in the early years.

Catch your child being polite when he or she:

- says "excuse me" after a sneeze
- holds open a door
- waits for a friend to catch up
- knocks for permission to enter through a closed door
- uses a quiet voice indoors

Joyfulness

Every child should feel a sense of joy. Although this has historically been a basic right and privilege of childhood, some children do not know the deep peace and security that comes with unconditional love and explodes with a joyful spirit. To live the biblical text "Always be joyful" (1 Thessalonians 5:16), a child must be totally and completely certain that God loves him and so do others in his life. Nurturing joy in the heart of a child is essential in today's trouble-filled world. Even when a child is disappointed, bored, or tired, he can still be joyful because he's certain that he's loved.

Catch your child being joyful when he or she:

- sings while getting dressed
- cheers up someone who is sad
- looks for a new friend after a friend moves away
- smiles at the first person he sees in the morning
- praises God and remembers that God loves him